ISBN-10: 1-936687-10-0
ISBN-13: 978-1-936687-10-7

Xerolage 50. First Edition published 2013 ISSN 1557-0983
Visual poetry, copy art & collage graphics, each issue devoted to the work of one artist. Xerolage is a word coined by mIEKAL aND to suggest the world of 8.5 x 11 art propagated by xerox technology. "The mimeo of the 80s." The primary investigation of this magazine is how collage technique of 20th century art, typography, computer graphics, visual & concrete poetry movements & the art of the xerox have been combined. 8.5x11, 24 pages each. Subscriptions $20/4 issues. For overseas delivery, add $15 for airmail printed matter.

Back issues $5.00 each.

Xexoxial Editions, 10375 Cty Hway Alphabet, LaFarge, WI 54639

www.xexoxial.org | perspicacity@xexoxial.org

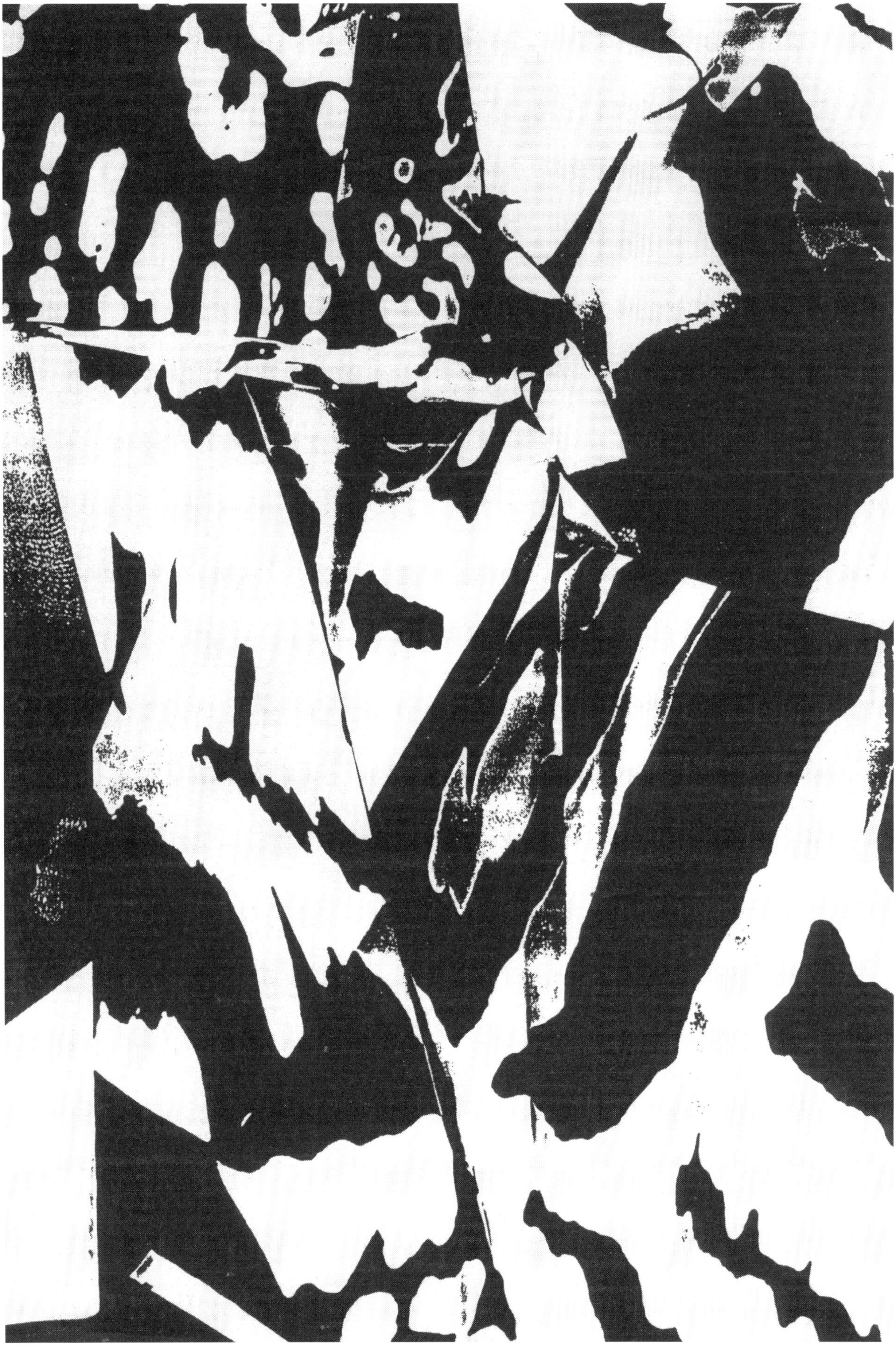

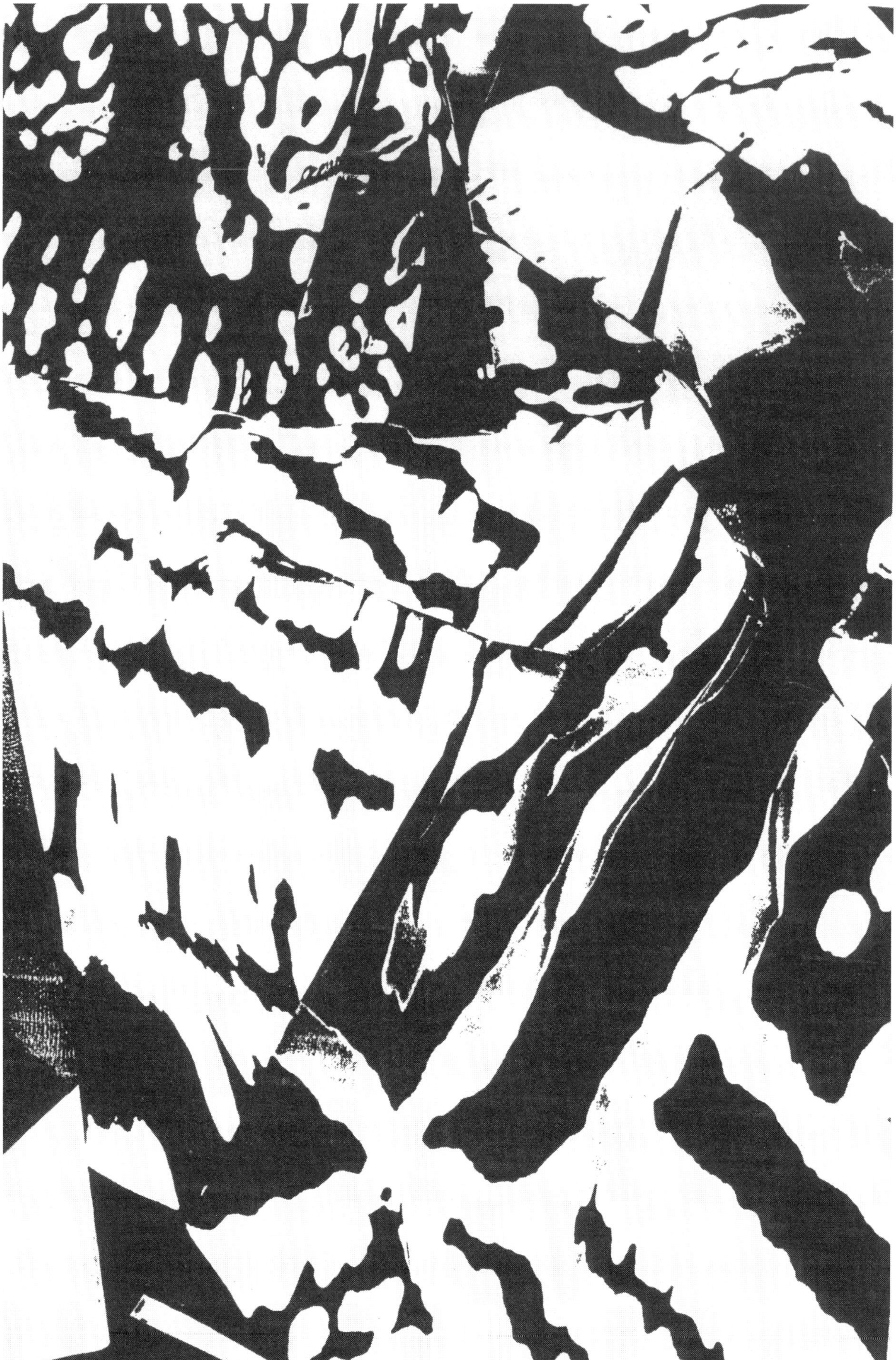

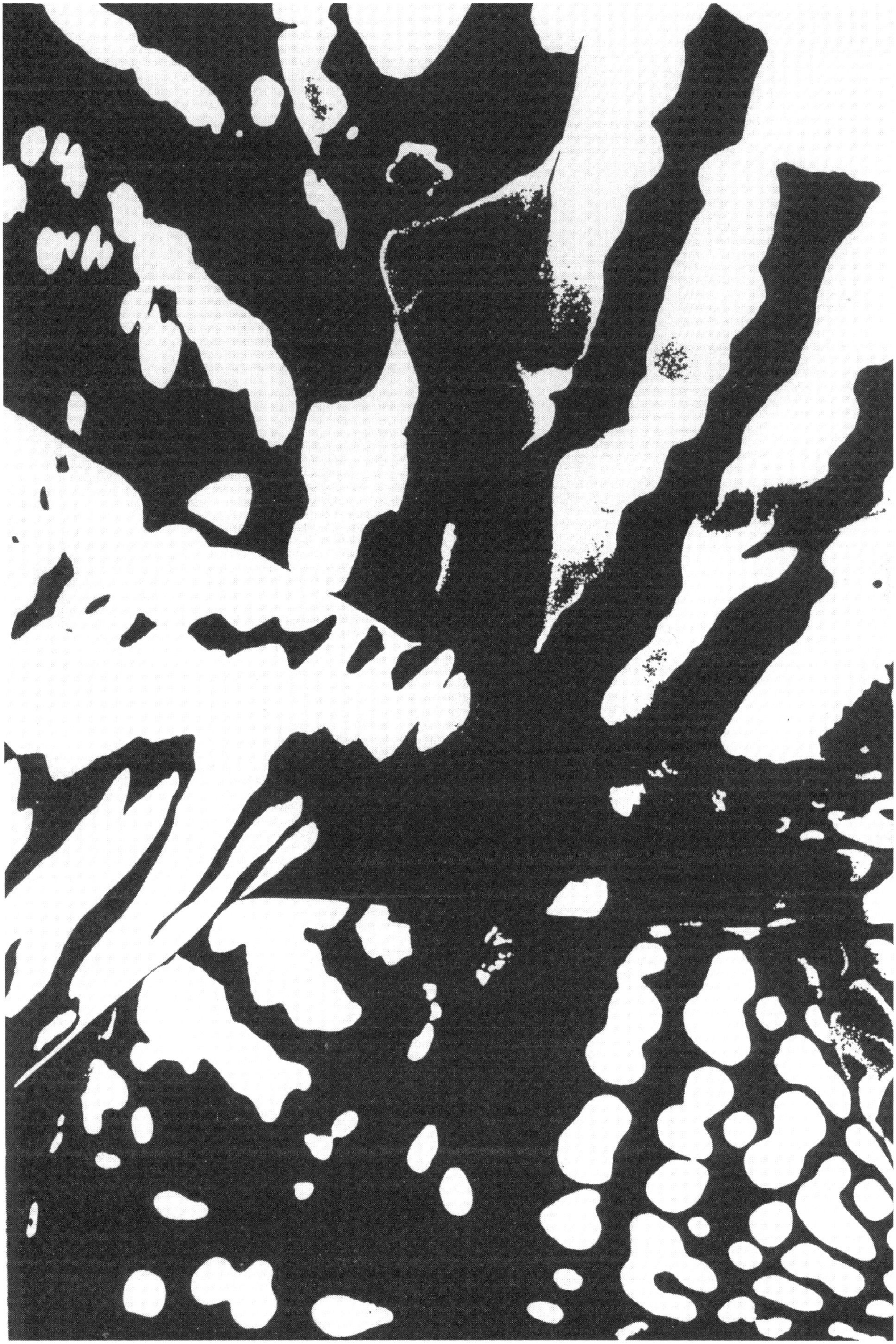

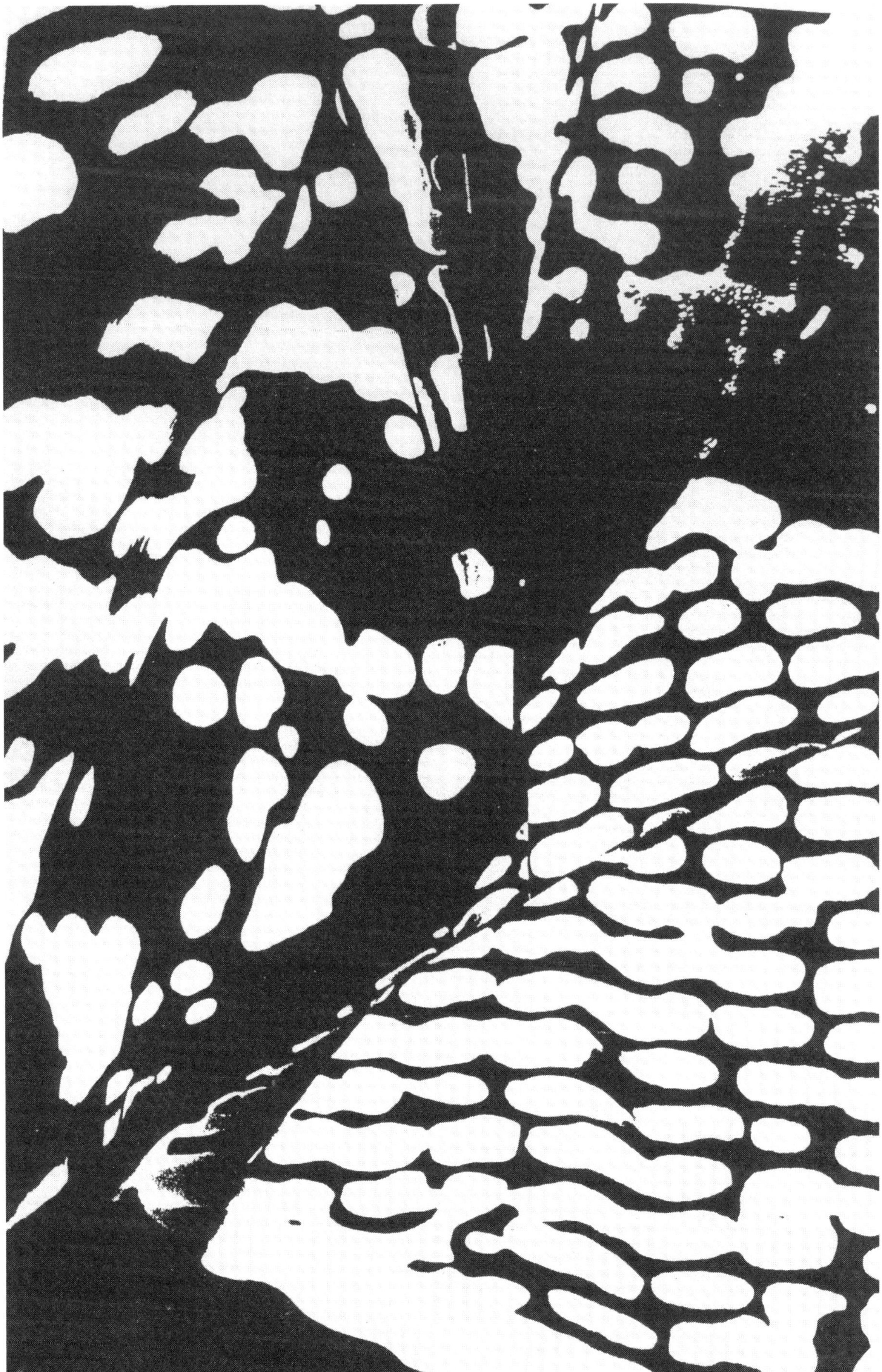

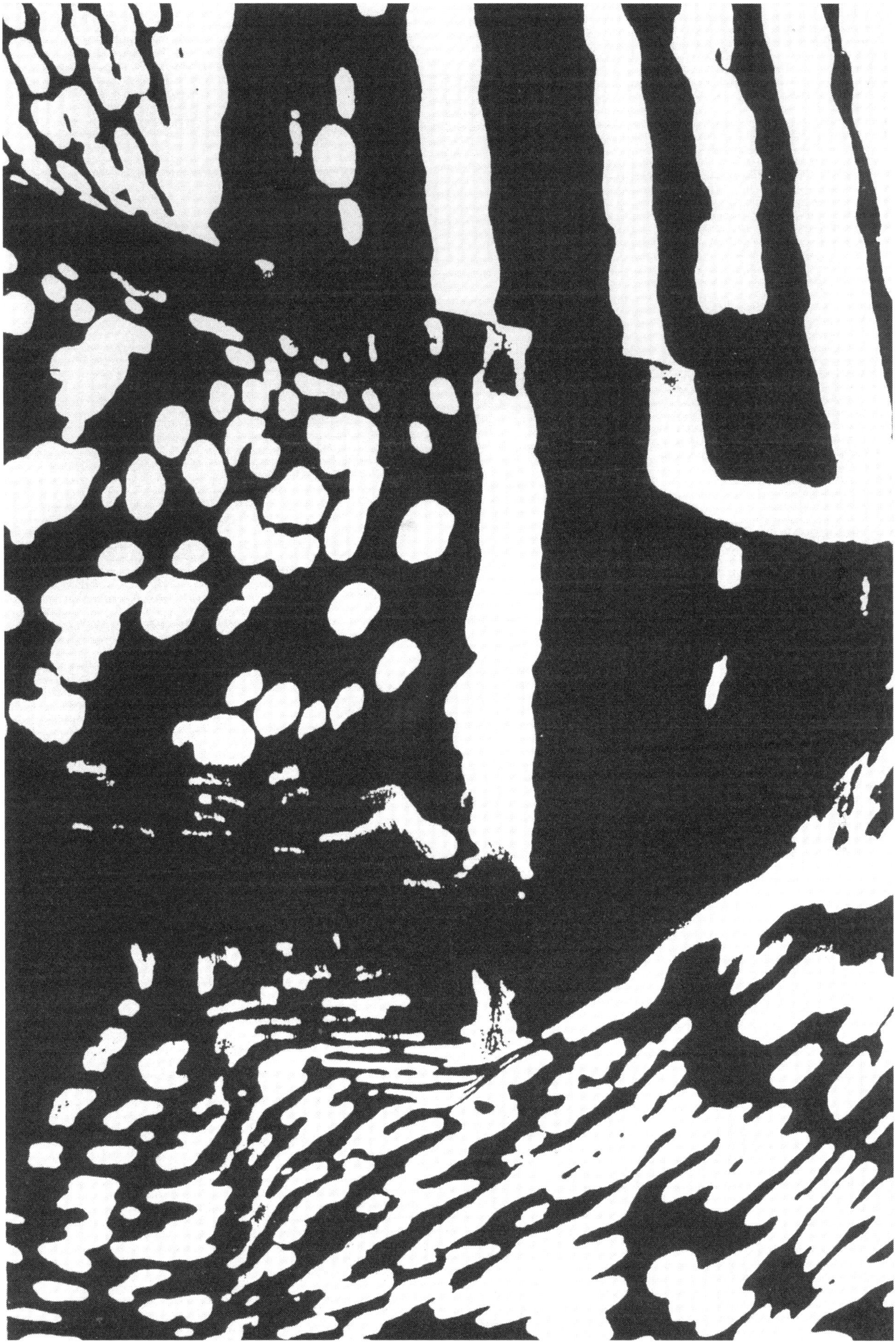

Bob Cobbing

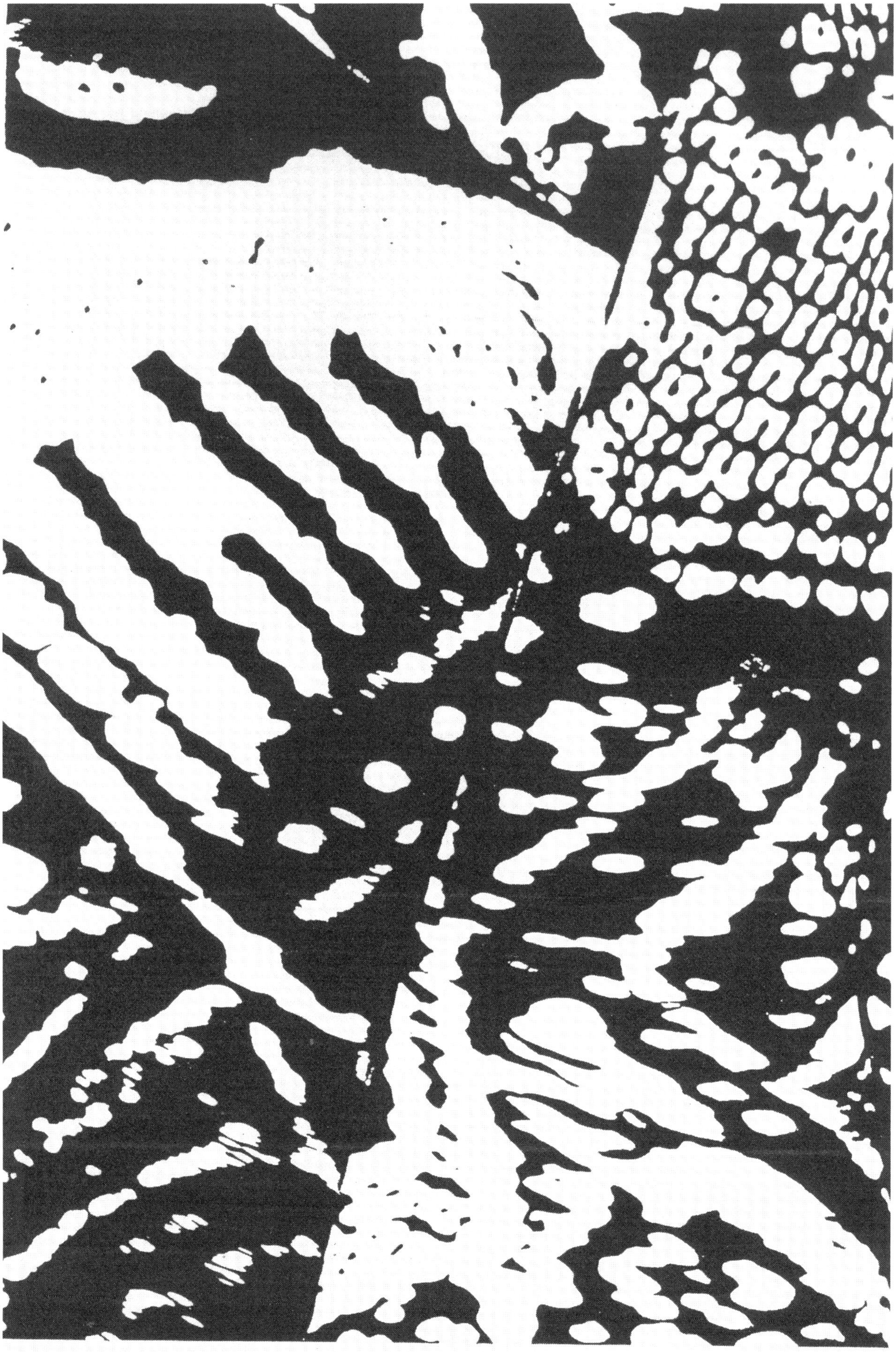

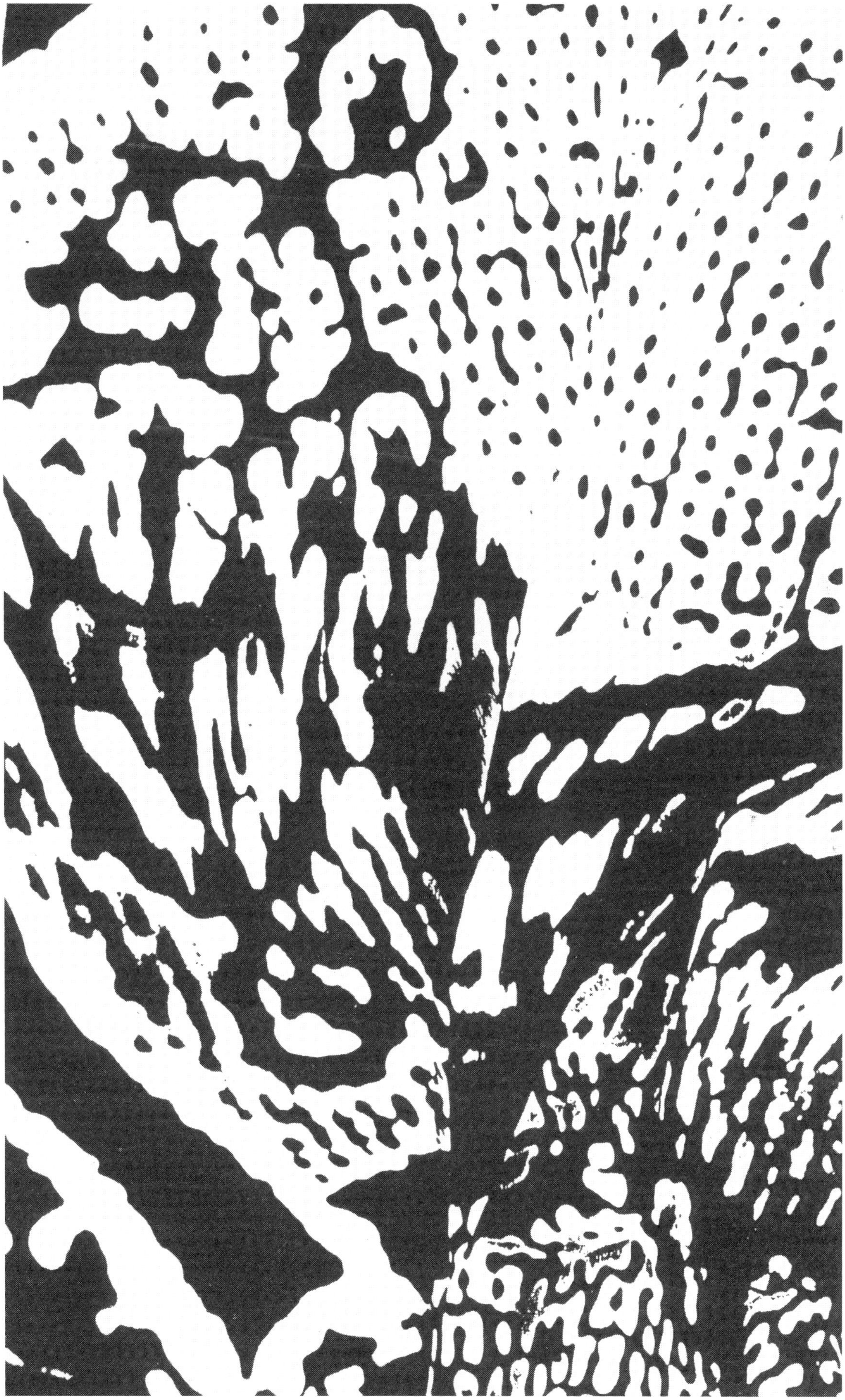

Bob Cobbing

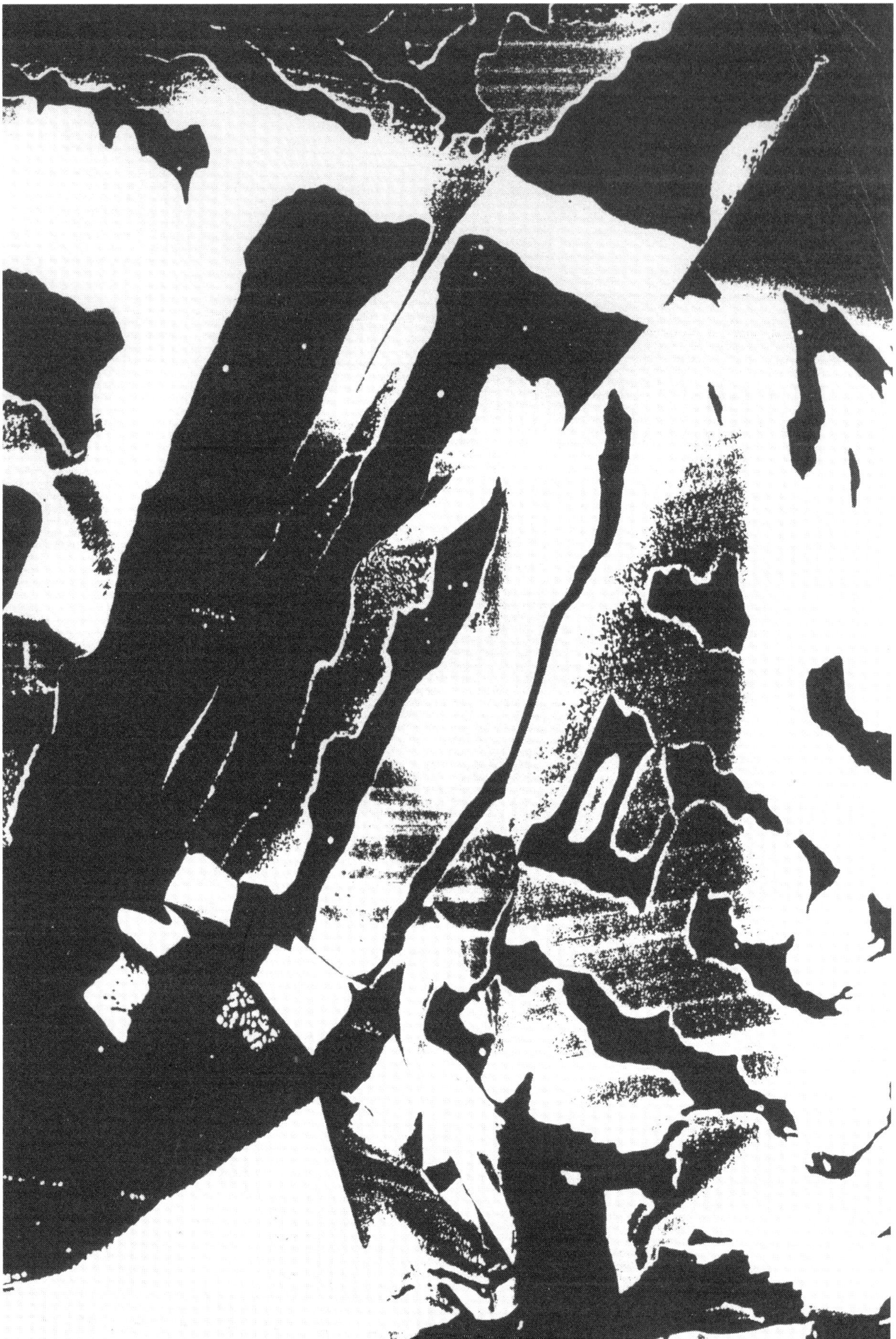

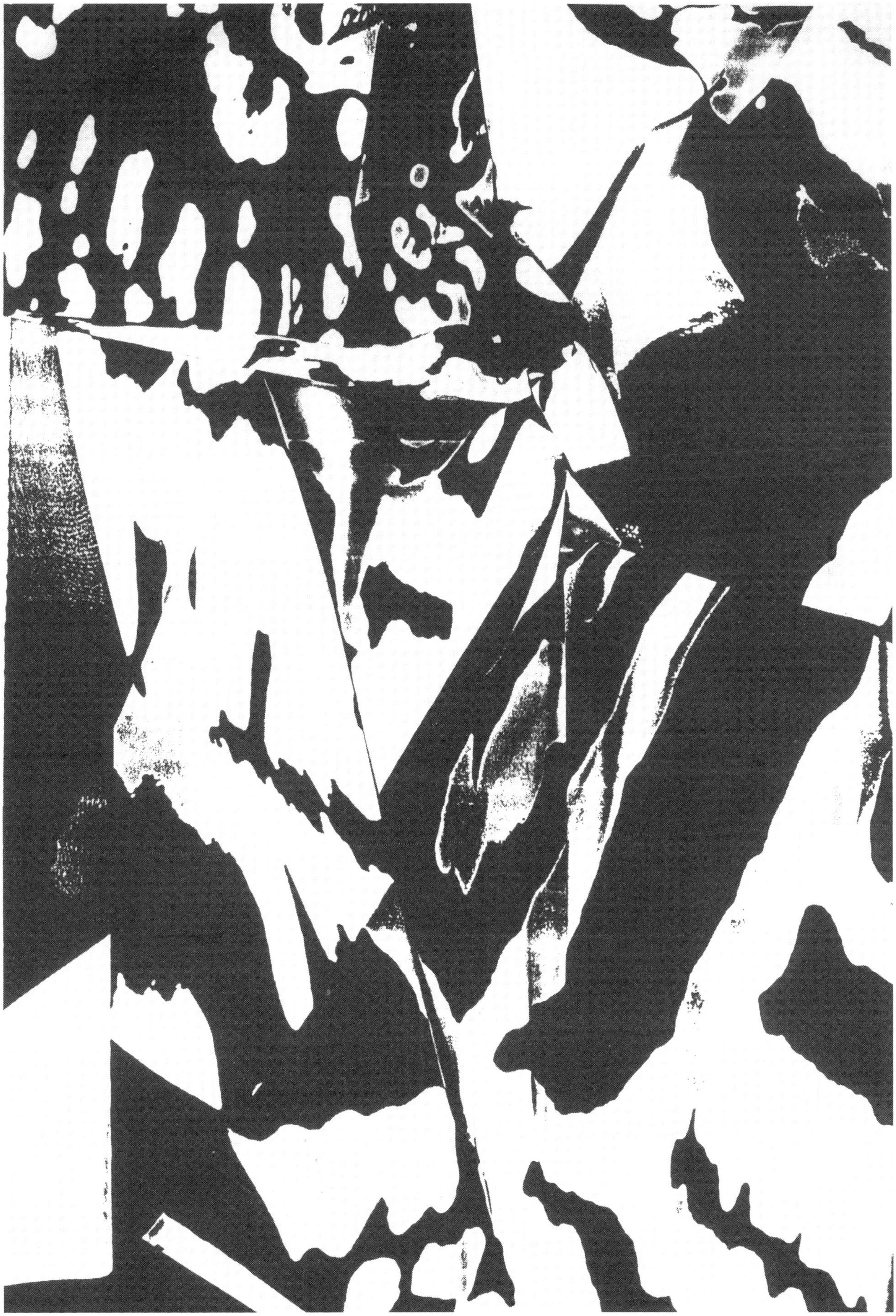

Bob Cobbing

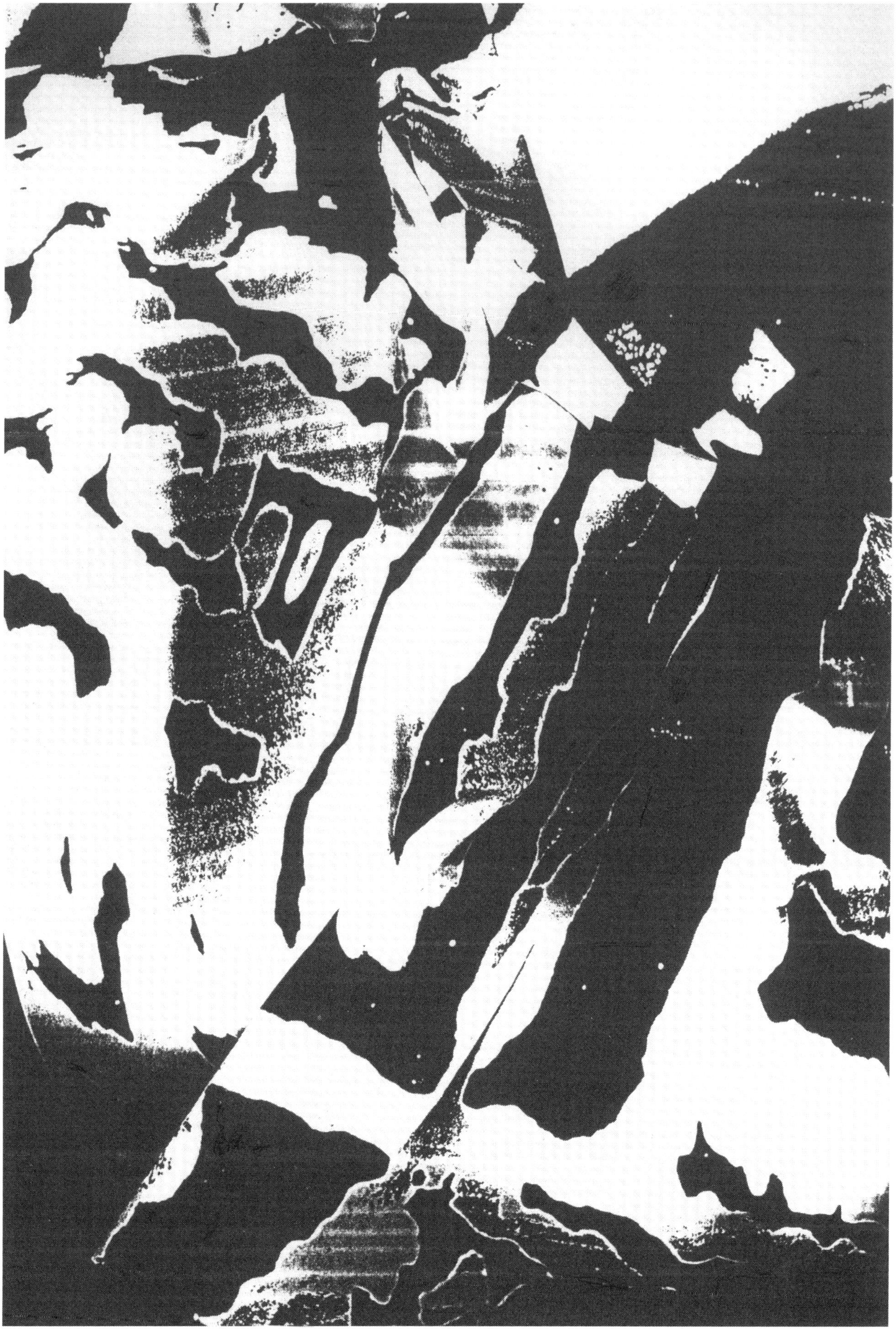

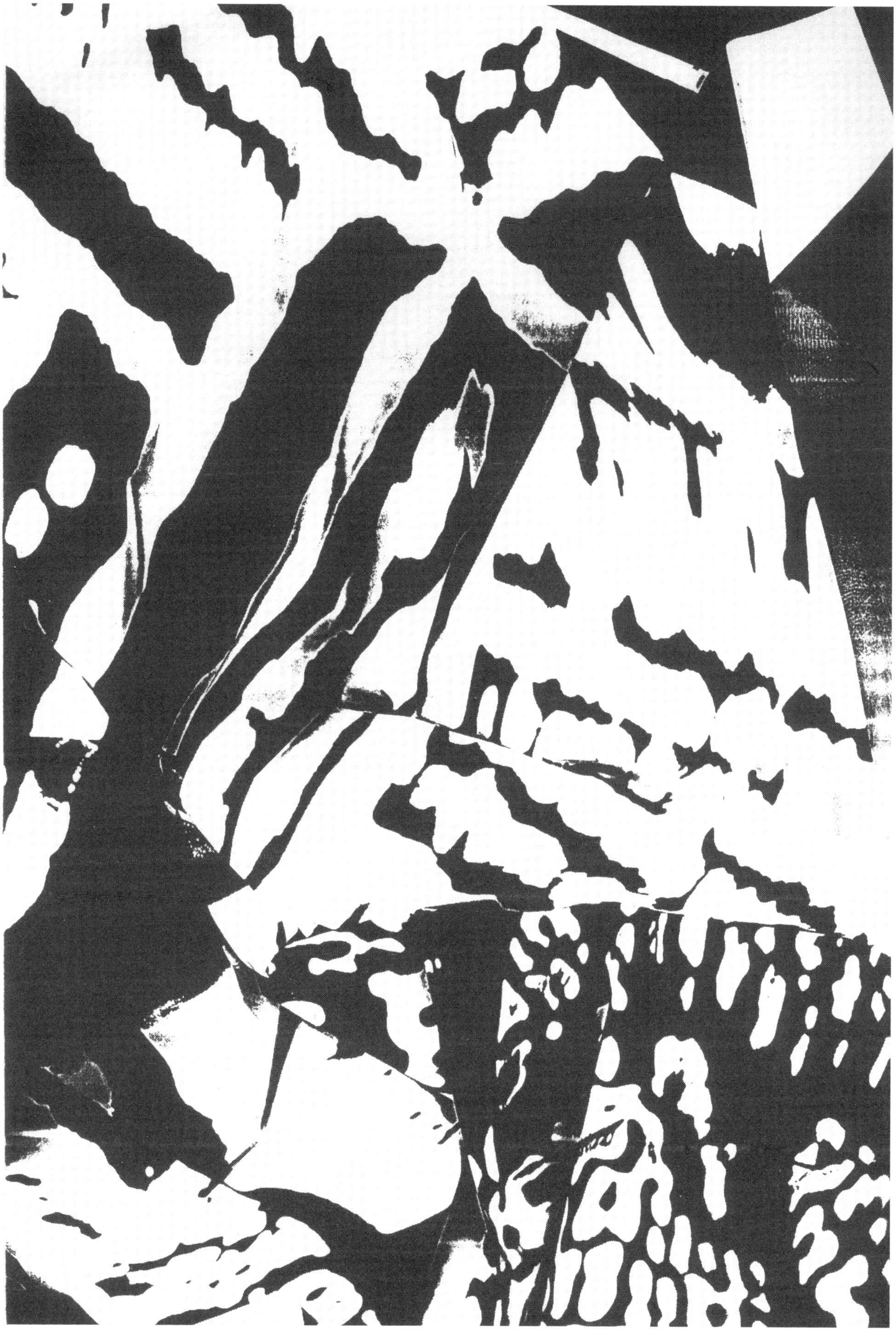

Bob Cobbing

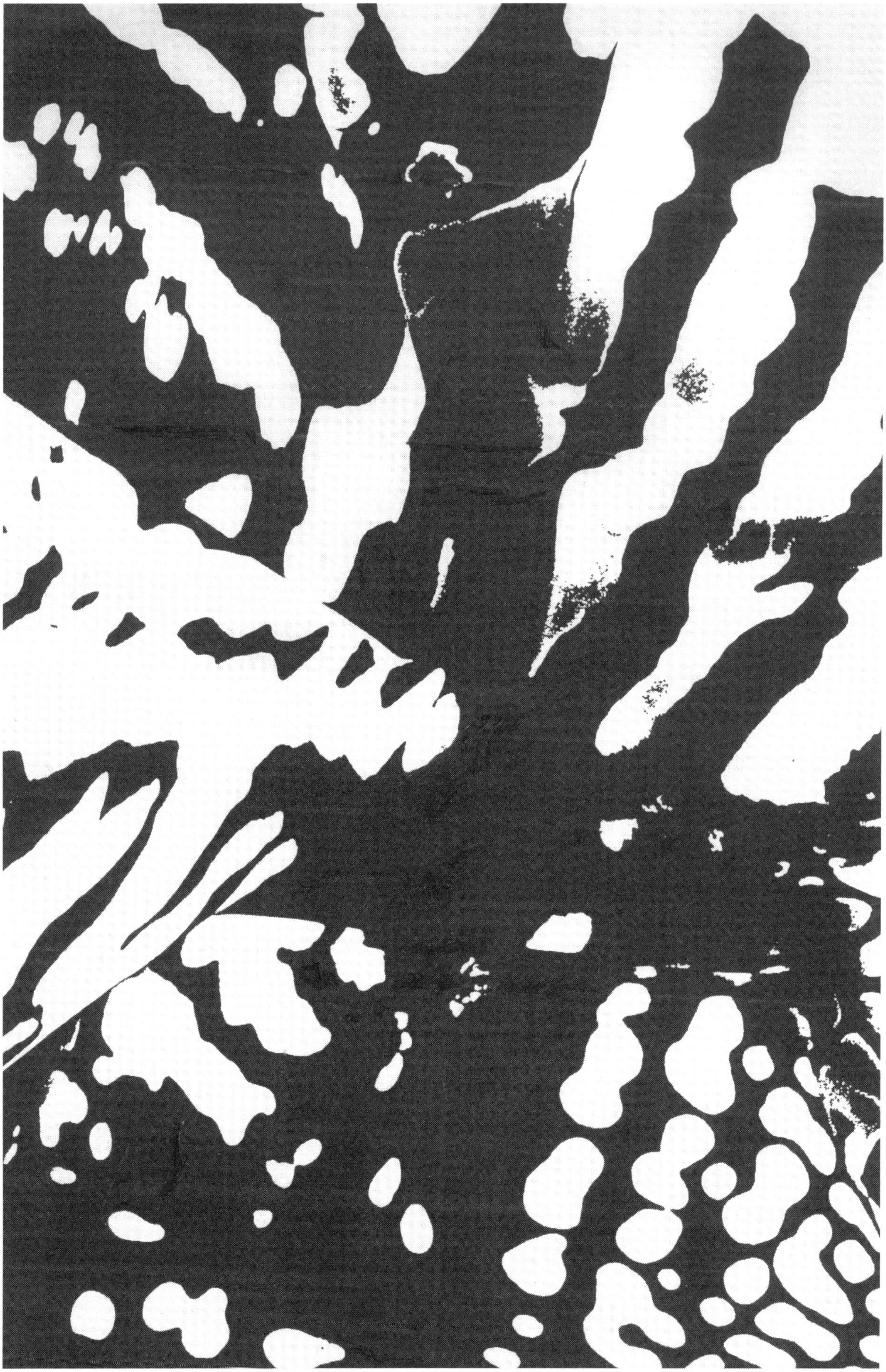

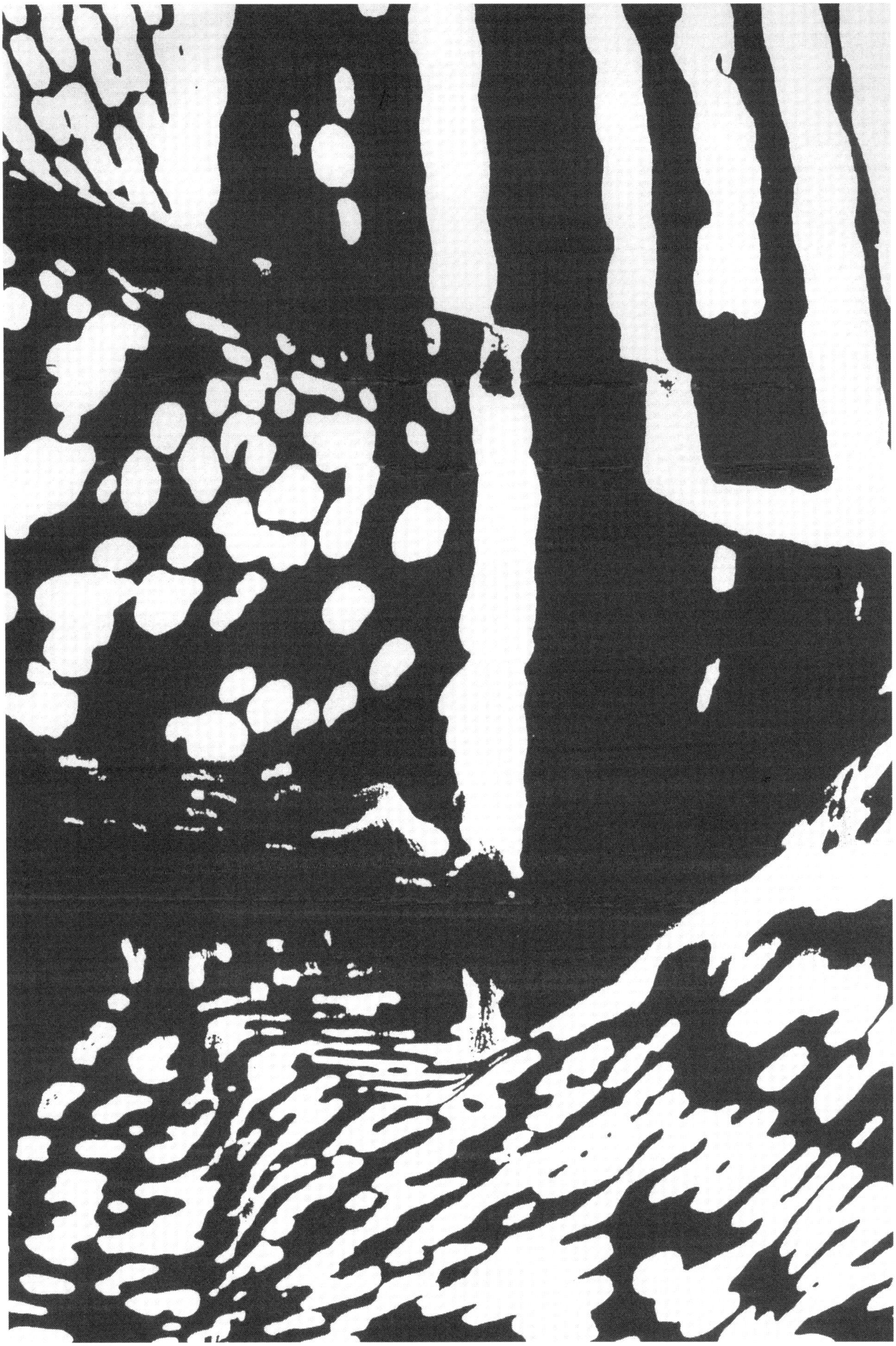

Bob Cobbing

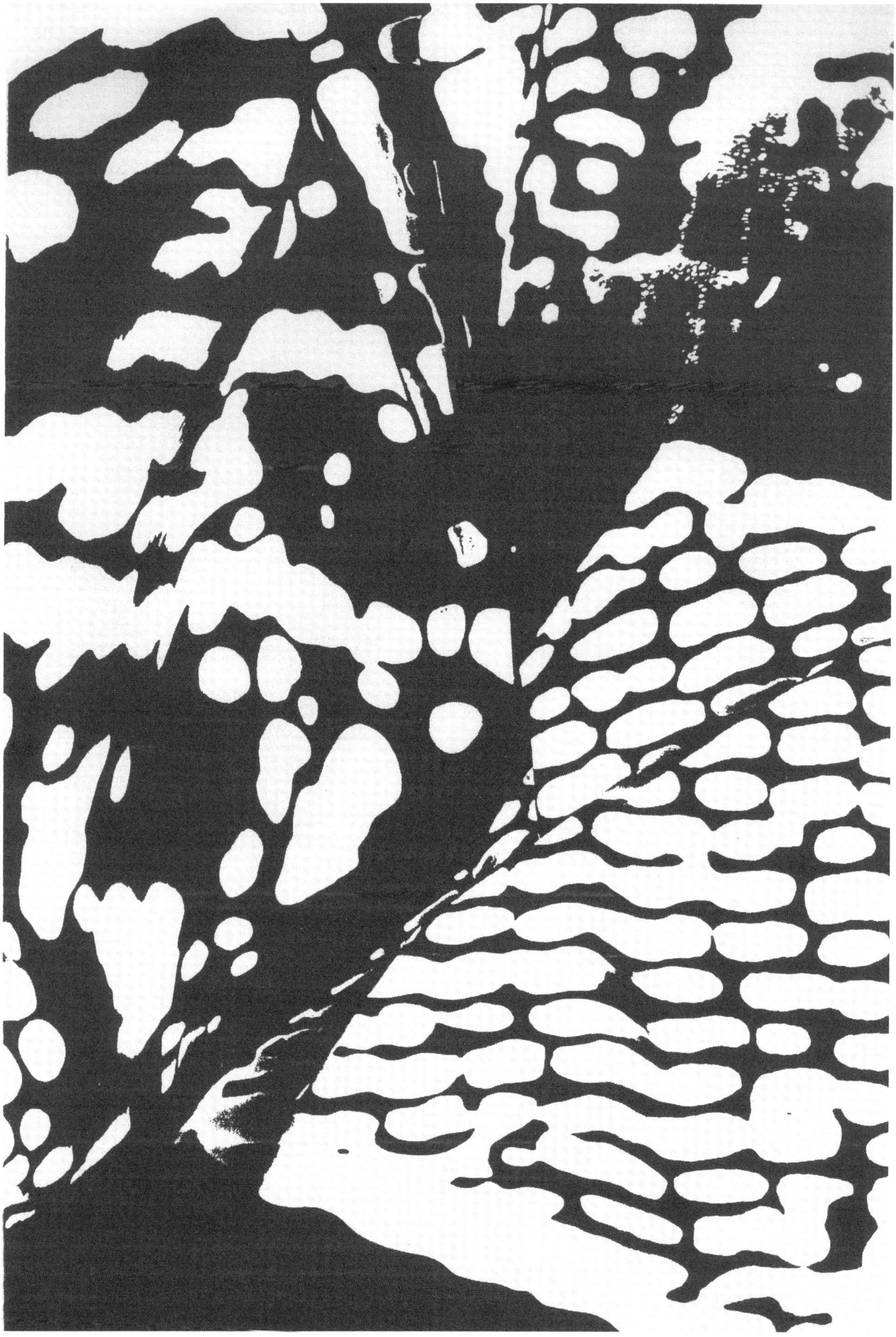

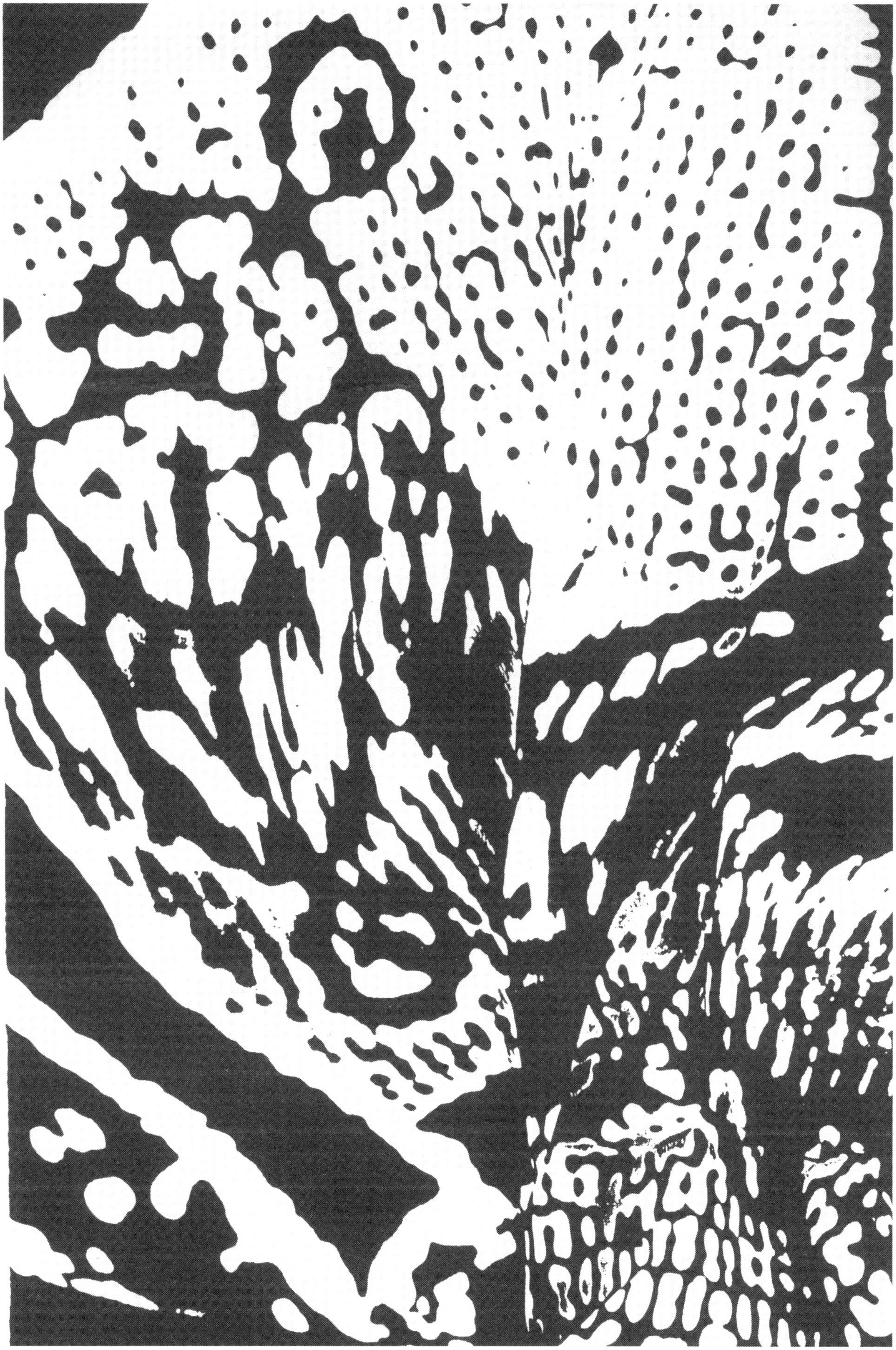

Bob Cobbing

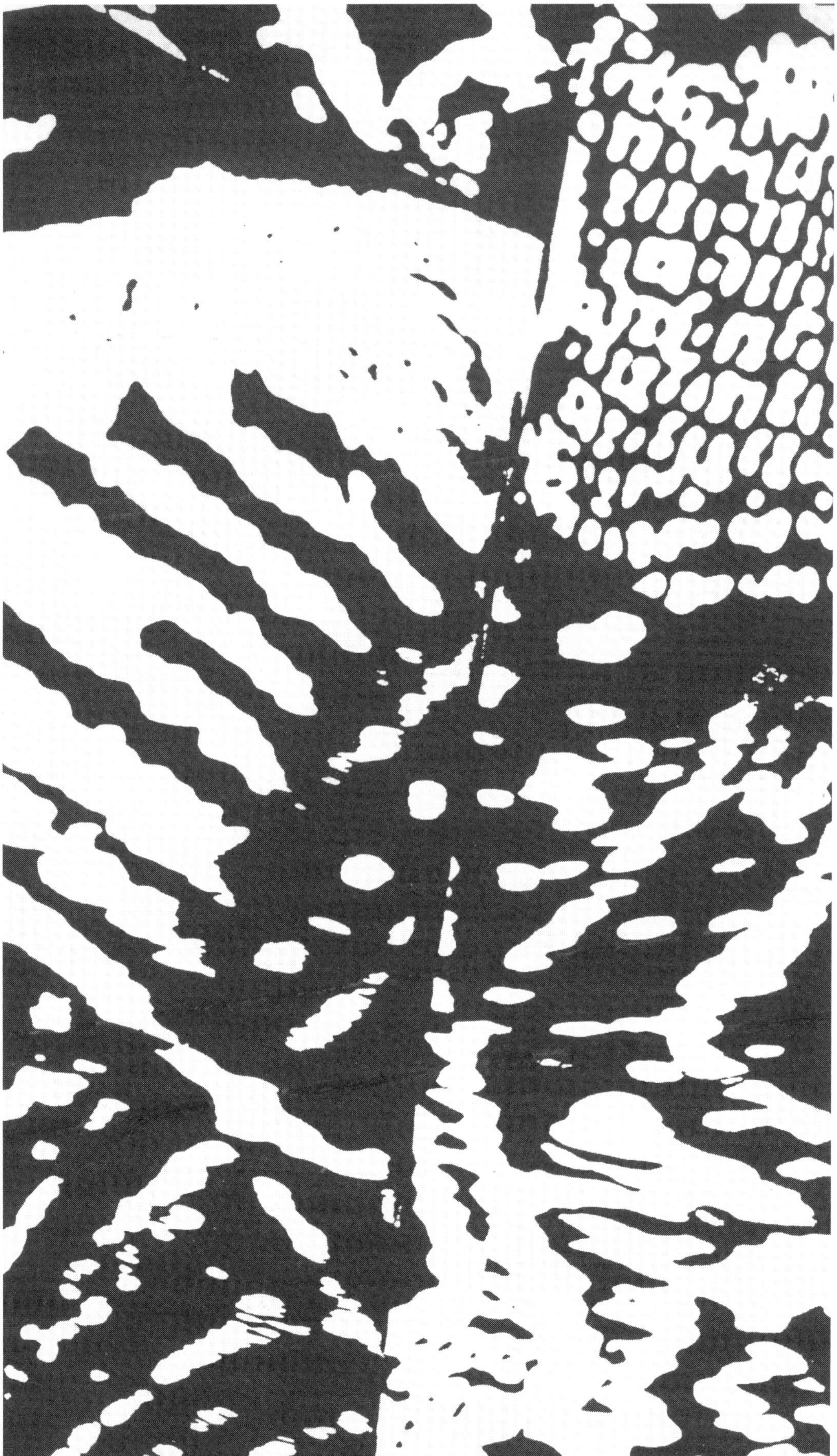

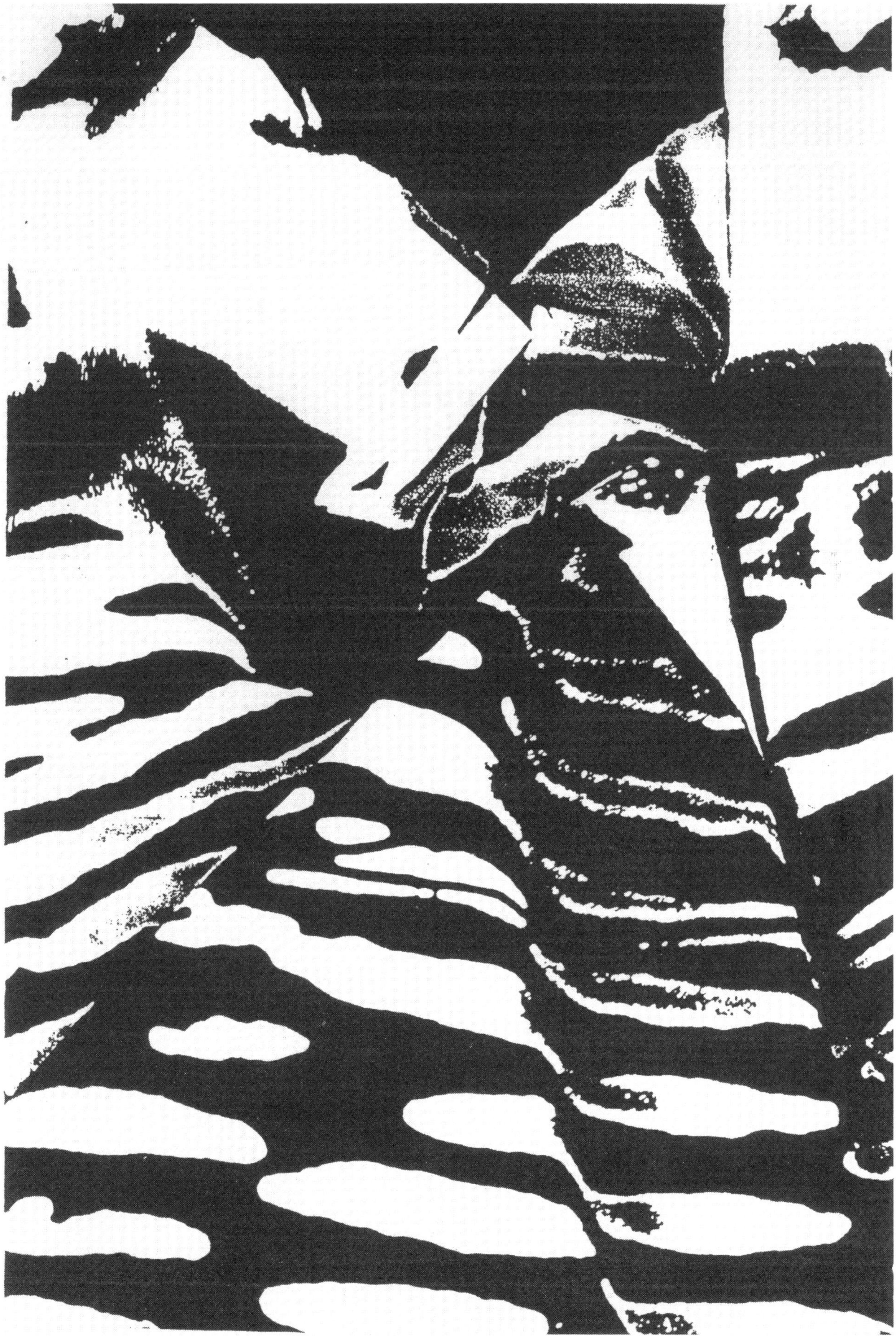

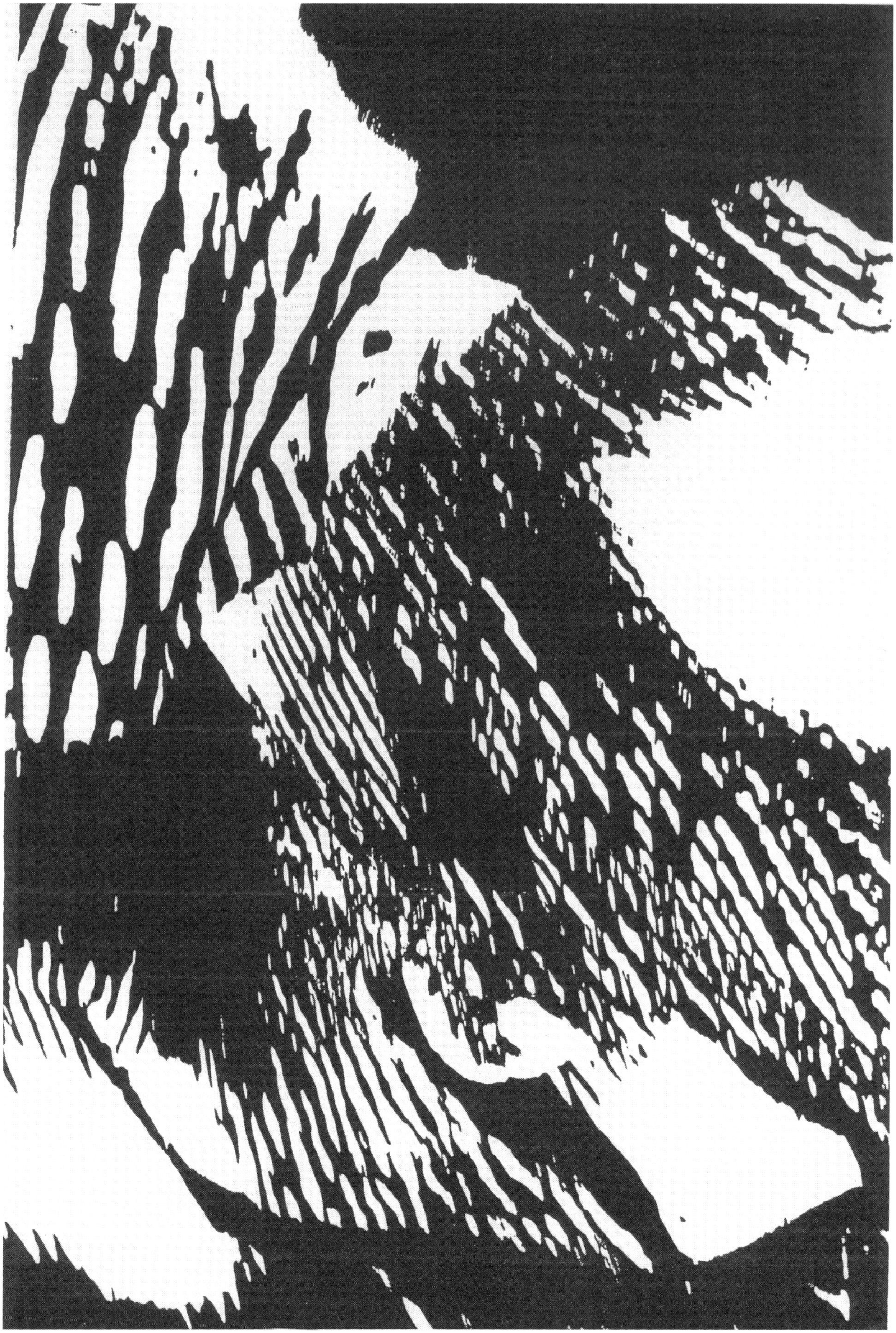

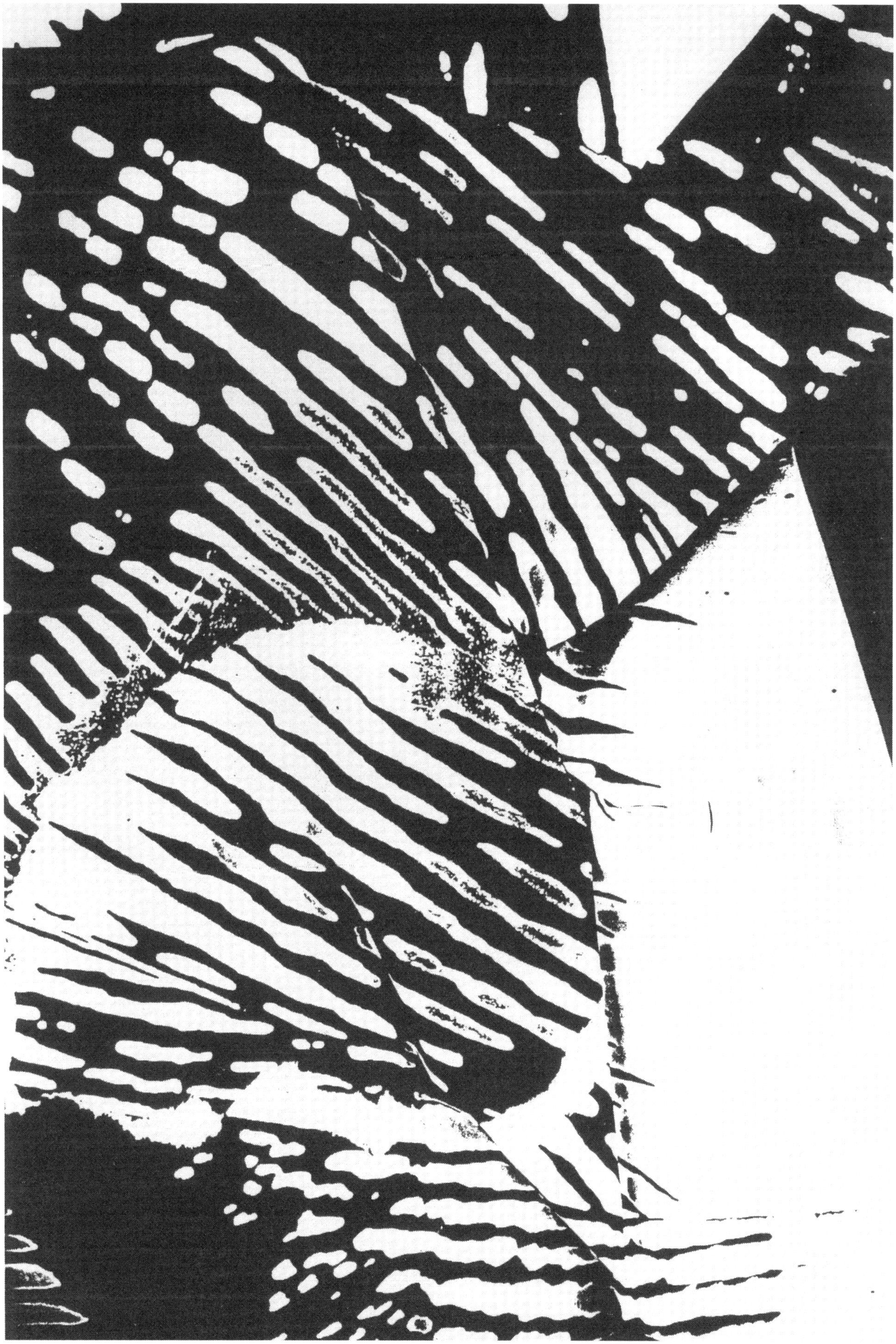

Bob Cobbing

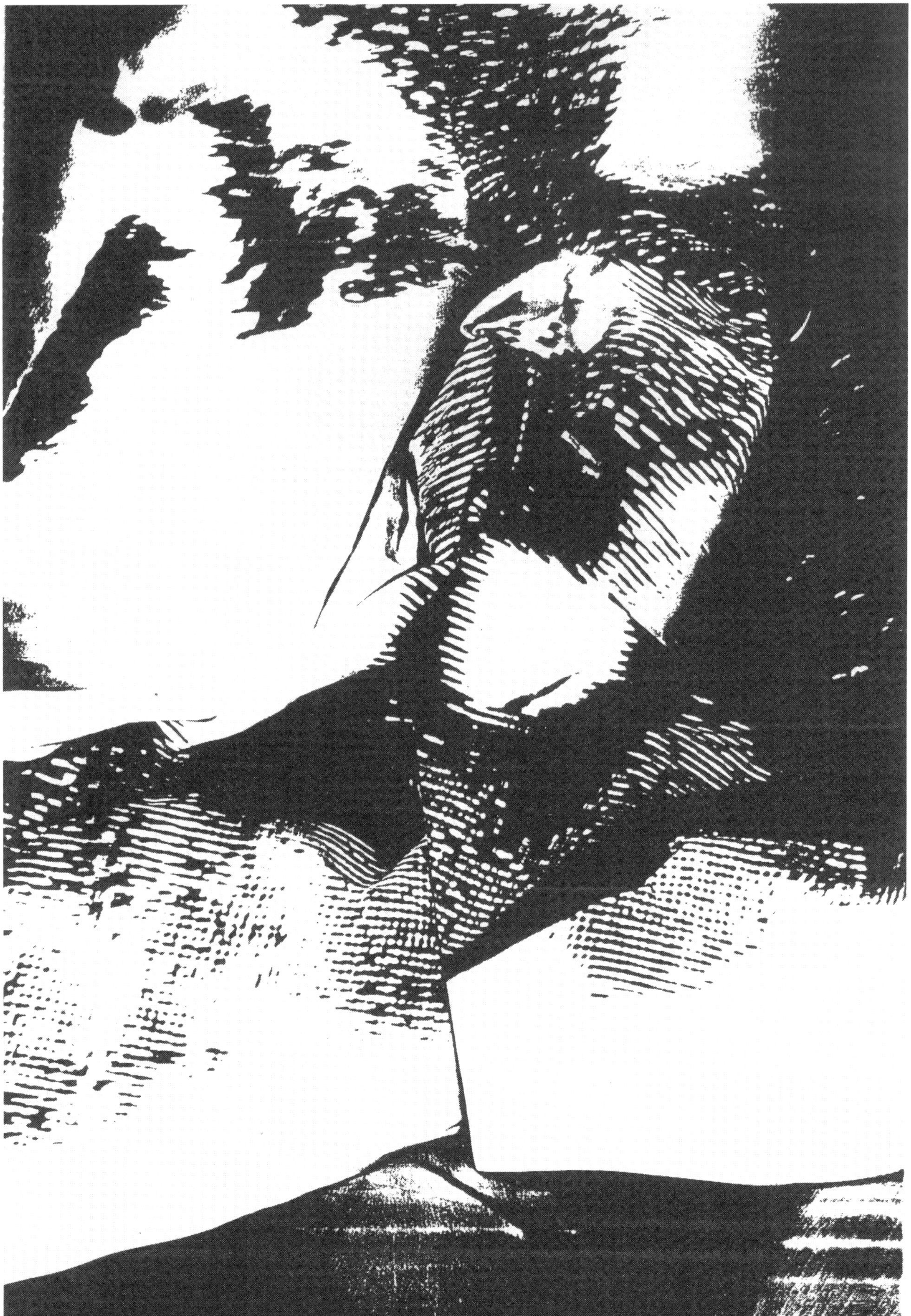

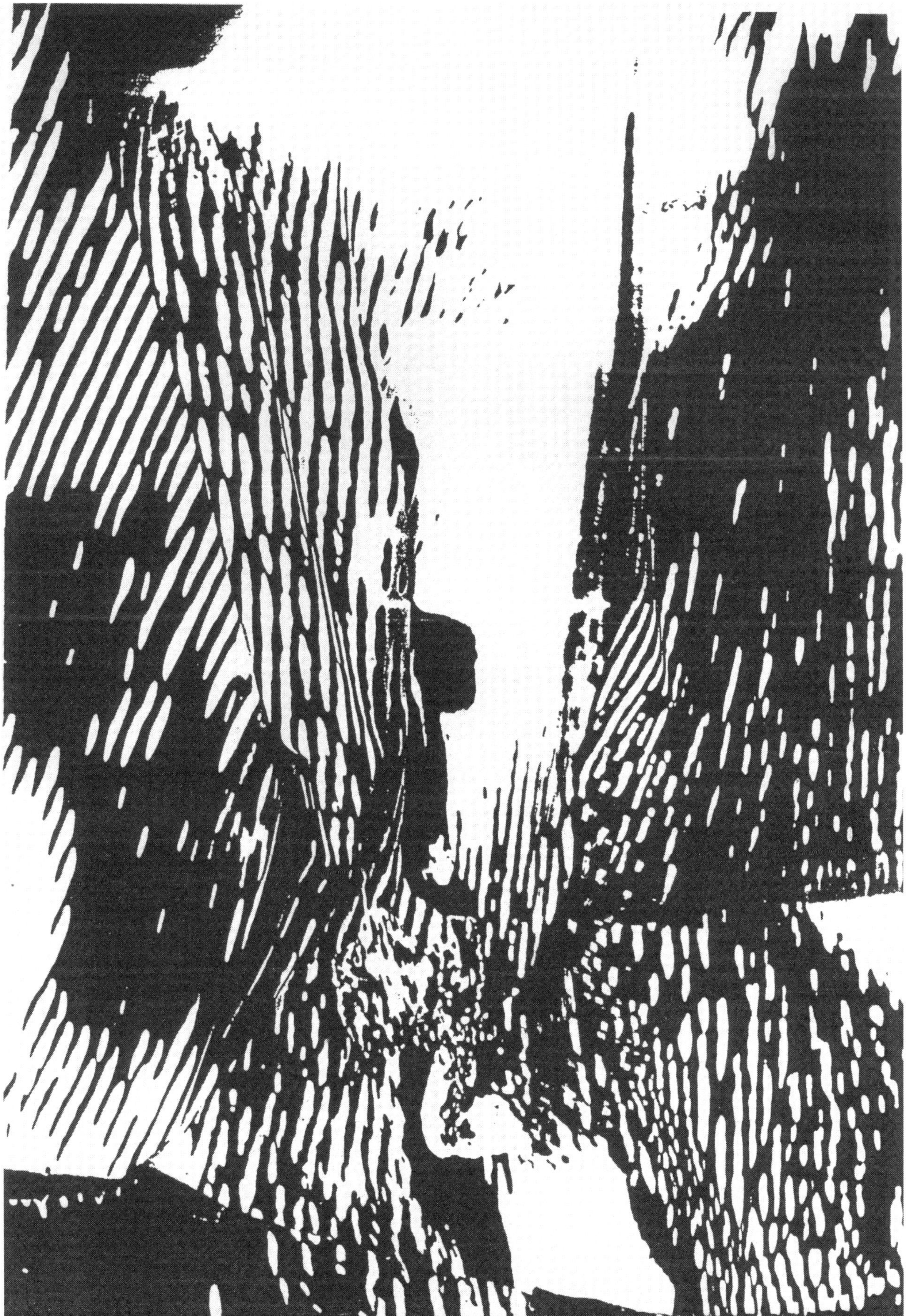

Bob Cobbing

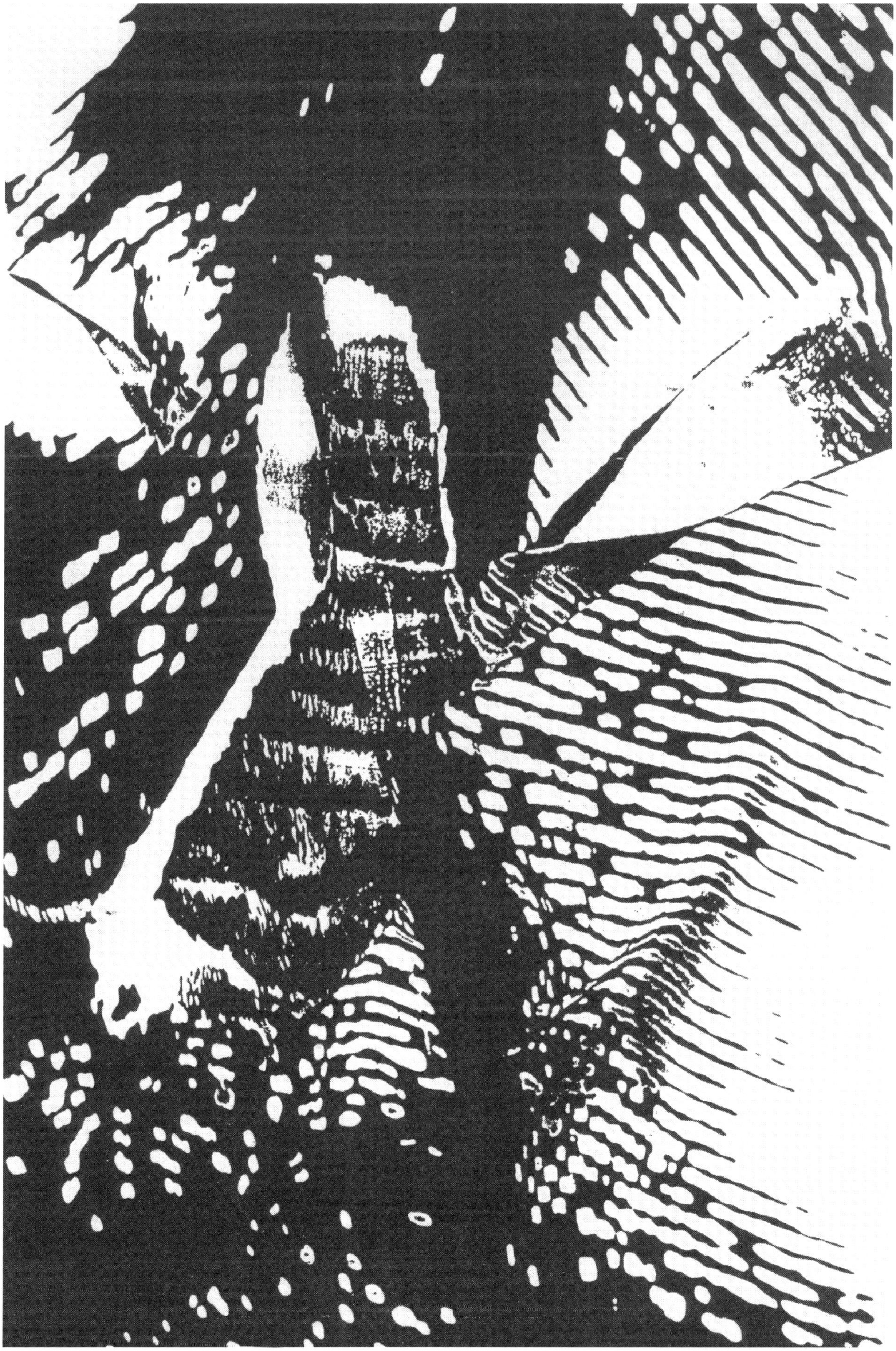

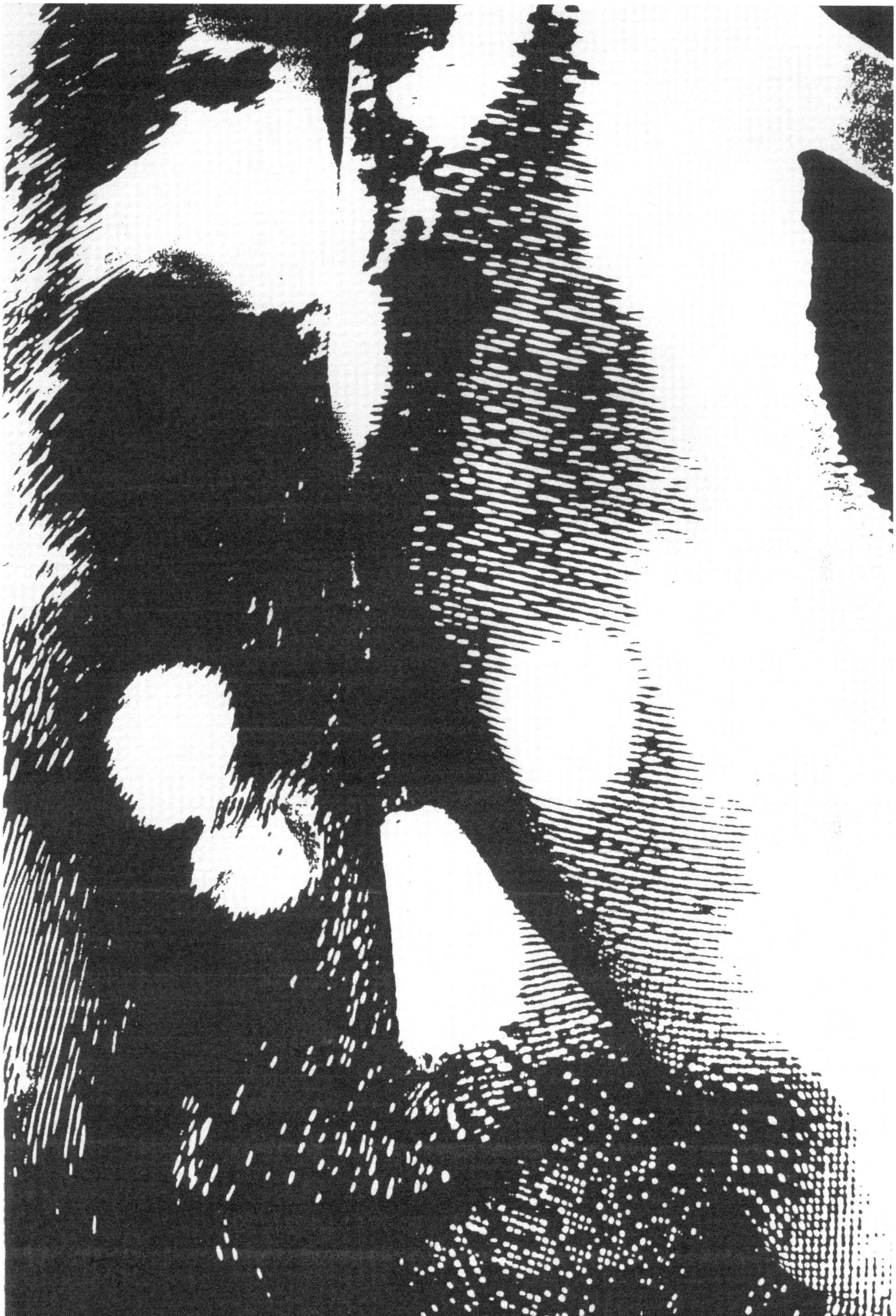

Bob Cobbing

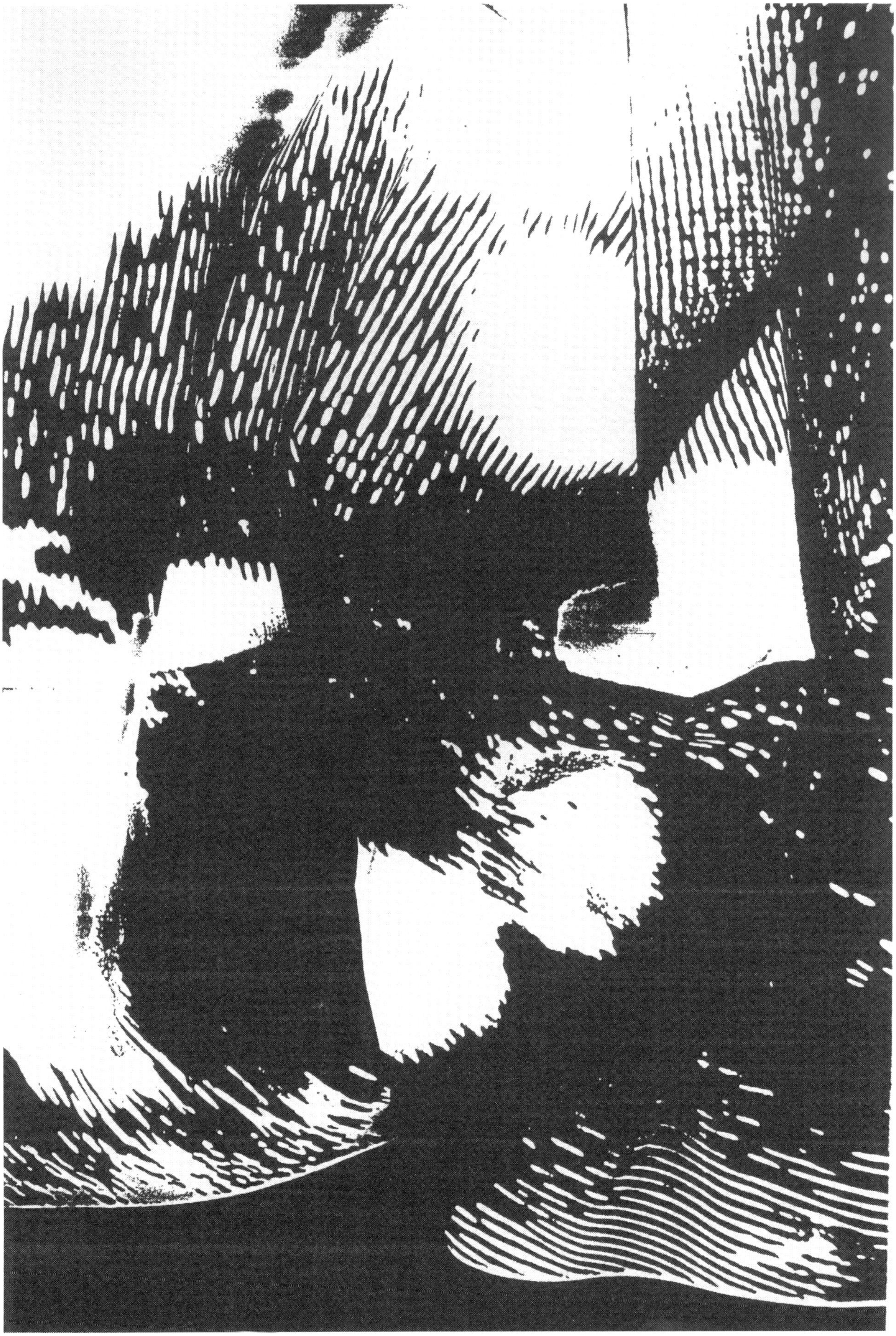

3 sequences by Bob Cobbing (1920 - 2002)

It is almost certain that these images have never been published before. Clearly, Cobbing valued the works: they are documented as to title and date in his hand-writing, on good quality laser prints; and he took care to preserve them.

The format is A4, a format, with A3, that he worked with throughout his last quarter century. Some works use other sizes, particularly B5 and B6; but generally that was achieved by trimming or photo-reduction. He composed usually on A4 and A3. Until the early 1980s, he had also used quarto (8 inches x 10 inches) and foolscap (17 inches x 13.5 inches), sometimes other "imperial sizes". In those days, his main writing and copying medium was the ink duplicator, if we exclude sound recording media. From 1984, he was a photocopy boy.

His image-composing methods were various. The ink duplication process provided multitudes of potential monotypes as by-product from ink-wet wax stencils. In both ink-duplication and photocopying (1984+), knowledge of how scanning transformed images played a large role, with and apart from papier collé. Photocopying also copes with moving objects on the glass platen.

A Cobbing original may tend towards the intangible. Output qualities, I should say "properties", varied depending where one was in the monthly copier maintenance cycle and where one was on the timeline towards machine obsolescence. He might reserve image(s) as print master(s) for future use while the rest of the print run was published. Then, at reprint, the print master might not be to hand and a copy was used. That copy might or might not be generationally identical to the missing master; or the copier might or might not do justice in some eyes to what it was copying. Yet, if the result satisfied Cobbing, simultaneously fastidious and tolerant, then that was that.

He declared that every one of his visual works was performable. So the images contained herein are both for you to look at and to perform. As notation, it is indicative rather than precise; but results can be remarkably close to each other if one utters with good will and honesty as well as intellectual rigour. Cobbing's term for that coherence was family resemblance.

Cobbing was, for decades, "the major exponent of concrete, visual and sound poetry in Britain. Long after its international heyday in the 1960s, he continued to produce visual texts that were also scores for performance (Robert Sheppard, **The Guardian**, Monday 7 October 2002). And the formal manner of those texts is a turmoil of new invention both in his solo writing and in his many collaborations.

Many speak of an enthusiasm for Poetry, but Cobbing was The Enthusiast: "Cobbing's legacy extends beyond his creative contribution to his support for creativity in seemingly endless forms and guises". (Scott Thurston, **Neon Highway 3**, 2003)

These pages. from a few months of a long creative life, their artist working relatively narrow samples of visual material, display understated variety in a factory of commotion and unexpected utterance. Cobbing is at an apogee and perigee in abstraction from and to the conventional linguistic sign; yet a few months later he will propose the inception of **Domestic Ambient Noise**, possibly his longest dialogue with another artist, perhaps among his most daring collaborative acts, stretching what could be done with concrete art. He was almost 74 years old at this point and still trying to get past himself!

Lawrence Upton
Goldsmiths, University of London
July 2010

Suggested further reading:

Bob Cobbing: and the book as medium:
http://www.bbk.ac.uk/readings/issues/issue4/upton_on_cobbing;

Lightsong 2 by Bob Cobbing:
http://www.lawrenceupton.org/reviews/lightsong.html

hot mazing on time:
http://www.pores.bbk.ac.uk/3/upton.html

Bob Cobbing: a worker in progress:
http://llpp.ms11.net/archive.html

Writers Forum: Life by 1000 Books in A Book of the Book
eds. Rothenberg & Clay; Granary Books, New York, 2001

[All above by Lawrence Upton]

Domestic Ambient Buoys in discussion with Alaric Sumner August 1999, London; Riding the Meridian ed. Ley) 1999;

Ballet Of The Speech Organs; Steven Ross Smith; Underwhich, Toronto 1998;

A prosthetics of poetry: the art of Bob Cobbing; Eric Mottram; Second Aeon 16-17; 1973

Visit wfuk.org.uk for details of availability of Cobbing's publications

Made in the USA
Monee, IL
04 November 2026

67379970R00018